READING SURVIVAL SKILLS

SURVIVAL SKILLS

FOR THE

MIDDLE GRADES

by Imogene Forte

Incentive Publications, Inc.
Nashville, Tennessee

Illustrated by Marta Drayton
Cover by Geoffrey Brittingham
Edited by Leslie Britt

ISBN 0-86530-279-0

PRINTED IN THE UNITED STATES OF AMERICA

TABLE OF CONTENTS

PREFACE vii

AUTHOR'S SAVVY (*Recognizing and Using Descriptive Words*) 9

AUTHOR'S SAVVY II (*Recognizing and Using Descriptive Words*) 10

A TRAGIC TALE (*Recognizing and Using Abbreviations*) 11

CONTRACTION FRACTIONS (*Using Contractions*) 12

PLURAL DECISIONS (*Recognizing and Using Plurals*) 13

POSITIVELY POSSESSIVES (*Recognizing and Using Possessives*) 14

HETTIE HARNESSES HETERONYMS (*Recognizing and Using Heteronyms*) 15

THE MEANING OF MATH (*Recognizing and Using Math Content Words*) 16

HERE'S LOOKING AT YOU (*Extending Personal Vocabulary*) 17

WORD CHEF (*Using the Dictionary*) 18

DINER'S KNOW-HOW (*Reading a Menu*) 19

FEELING FINDERS (*Associating Words with Feelings*) 20-21

SHOW YOUR FEELINGS (*Associating Words with Feelings*) 22

BIRDS OF A FEATHER DO WHAT? FLOCK TOGETHER!
(*Interpreting Idiomatic Expressions*) 23

TIME ON THE LINE (*Recalling Information and Selecting Facts To Remember*) 24

FRONT PAGE REVIEW (*Finding Answers to Specific Questions*) 25-26

FUNNEL YOUR READING (*Using Key Words, Phrases, and Topic Sentences
To Understand Main Ideas*) 27-28

PEERING AT PARAGRAPHS (*Recognizing Main Ideas*) 29

DETAIL DEDUCTION (*Reading To Find Details*) 30

ANALOGIES ON DEPOSIT (*Making Word Associations*) 31

SPECIAL NEWS WATCH (*Understanding/Summarizing Main Ideas*) 32-33

FISHY FACTS FILMSTRIPS (*Summarizing*) 34-35

ABSOLUTELY ACCURATE ANSWERS (*Reading To Verify Answers*) 36-37

WHAT WILL HAPPEN? (*Drawing Conclusions*) 38

AESOP'S WORKSHOP (*Making Inferences*) 39

PREDICTION PUZZLES (*Predicting Outcomes*) 40

THE RIGHT THING TO DO (*Making Value Judgments*) 41

IDENTIFY THE IRRELEVANTS (*Distinguishing Between Relevant and Irrelevant Information*) 42

ARE YOU SURE ABOUT THAT? (*Distinguishing Between Fact and Opinion*) 43

OPINIONATED STATEMENTS (*Distinguishing Between Fact and Opinion*) 44

GET THE POINT! (*Distinguishing Between Fact and Opinion*) 45

MOOD MINDED (*Understanding Author's Purpose*) 46

I'D RATHER SEE ONE THAN BE ONE! (*Visualizing*) 47

DISCONCERTING DICTIONARIES (*Using the Dictionary*) 48

QUESTIONS TO ANSWER (*Using Reference Materials To Find Answers to Specific Questions*) 49-50

RELEVANT REFERENCES (*Using Multiple References To Locate Information*) 51

TOWERING THESAURUS (*Using the Thesaurus*) 52-53

HIGH-FLYING FLAGS (*Using the Encyclopedia*) 54-55

CARD CATALOG COGITATION (*Using the Card Catalog*) 56-57

WORD ROUND-UP (*Using Newspapers and Magazines*) 58

AN INDEX INDICATES (*Using an Index*) 59

GLANCING AT THE GLOSSARY (*Using the Glossary*) 60

PIN A PLACE (*Using a Map To Check Known Facts*) 61-62

ALL ABOUT AUSTRALIA (*Reading a Map*) 63

WORLDLY WISE (*Reading a Globe*) 64

BENJY'S BEST BET (*Reading a Chart*) 65

GRAPH GAZING (*Reading a Graph*) 66

LOST IN PUNCTUATION FOREST (*Using Punctuation*) 67

OUTLINES CAN GO AROUND AND AROUND (*Outlining/Organizing Ideas*) 68-69

CONSIDER THE SOURCE (*Taking Notes from Reading*) 70

A QUICK ONCE-OVER (*Skimming To Locate Information*) 71

AN INSIDE LOOK AT BOOKS (*Developing Reading Independence*) 72-73

ON THE LOOKOUT FOR WORDS (*Developing Reading Independence*) 74

LIBRARY SURVEY (*Rating Reading Interests*) 75

READING KNOW-HOW (*Developing Reading Accuracy*) 76

ANSWER KEYS 77-79

PREFACE

Teachers, administrators, and others responsible for planning and implementing programs for middle grades students realize the need to help them develop and use effective reading skills. Perhaps of more significance, they see that the educational system is charged with the task of helping these youngsters recognize the importance of reading proficiency in their everyday lives. Unfortunately, many adolescents reacting to the media-saturated world of hi-tech, high expectations, and high pressure tend to view computers, telephones, and audio/video devices as replacements for pencil, paper, books, and even conversation as a means of communicating ideas and information. It is imperative that young adults be taught that reading skills provide the most solid foundation for success in the Information Age.

This book has been developed to provide middle grades students with a series of practical skills-based exercises which promote reading proficiency. Its purpose is to familiarize students with the kinds of reading tasks they will confront on a daily basis and facilitate their survival as young adults in an increasingly aggressive and highly competitive world. In accordance with whole language theory and approach, these activities are designed to integrate the fundamental skills of reading, writing, thinking, and speaking and to link reading activities to real-life experiences in order to enhance comprehension.

The format is skill-oriented and includes both teacher-directed and self-directed student activities. The design is "user-friendly"— it is written to the user and presented in a simple, sequential style requiring little outside preparation. The activities are based on topics of high interest and relevance to today's middle graders. They are designed to capture attention and challenge the imagination of students of this age, encourage more efficient and effective work habits, and result in improvement in the use of functional language skills and reading proficiency.

Make this story livelier by replacing the words or phrases underlined in the story with words from the list below. Rewrite the story on a separate sheet of paper with the word substitutions. Use each word only once, and circle it so you will know it has been used. Finally, give the story a more exciting title, and illustrate it.

THE EMPTY HOUSE

When Alicia <u>found</u> that she was <u>by herself</u> in the <u>big</u>, <u>empty</u> <u>house</u>, her heart began to <u>beat quickly</u>. She <u>called</u> for help, but her only <u>answer</u> was a <u>strange</u> <u>quiet</u>. Her <u>walk</u> <u>echoed</u> as she <u>moved</u> through the <u>empty</u> hallway to the <u>top</u> of the stairs. She <u>stopped</u> and tried to <u>look</u> through the <u>white</u> <u>fog</u> that filled the <u>house</u> to see what was at the <u>bottom</u> of the <u>stairs</u>, but everything was <u>foggy</u>. Her legs <u>shook</u> as she <u>made</u> herself <u>walk down</u> the stairs. When she <u>came to</u> the landing, she <u>sat</u> down to rest. She was too <u>scared</u> to go <u>on</u>. <u>Then</u> something <u>dark</u> moved at the <u>bottom</u> of the <u>stairs</u>. Alicia was too <u>afraid</u> to <u>take a breath</u>. She heard something <u>coming</u> toward her, something that had <u>sharp</u> <u>feet</u> that clicked on <u>every</u> step. She <u>pushed</u> against the <u>railing</u>. Whatever it was had <u>just about</u> <u>found</u> her. She heard a <u>quiet</u> <u>sound</u> and felt something <u>cold</u> <u>run</u> over her arm. <u>Afraid of</u> the worst, she <u>looked</u> up <u>finally</u>, and then <u>put</u> out her arms. A warm <u>furry</u> body climbed into her lap and <u>licked</u> her shoulder. Alicia <u>laughed</u> out loud. It was her own <u>dog</u> Oscar. She wasn't <u>by herself</u> anymore. She and Oscar <u>got</u> up and <u>ran</u> down the rest of the <u>steps</u> and out the front door into the <u>daylight</u>. They were <u>fine</u> at last!

WORD LIST

deserted	farther	at last	eerie
giggled	trail	forced	reverberated
footsteps	nails	paused	frightened
pointed	peeked	crept	indistinct
alone	raced	reply	stairway
suddenly	almost	each	terrified
jumped	to descend	nuzzled	mansion
vacant	sank	abode	shadowy
fuzzy	safe	icy	trembled
reached	low	steps	staircase
pound	sunshine	fearing	ghostly
breathe	moving	head	discovered
silence	puppy	foot	screamed
banister	base	peer	
snarl	isolated	mist	
realized	shrank	held	

Name _____ Date _____

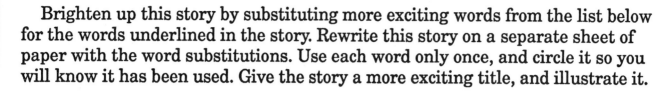

AUTHOR'S SAVVY II

Brighten up this story by substituting more exciting words from the list below for the words underlined in the story. Rewrite this story on a separate sheet of paper with the word substitutions. Use each word only once, and circle it so you will know it has been used. Give the story a more exciting title, and illustrate it.

A JUNGLE TRIP

As the <u>group</u> went into the <u>deep</u> jungle for a nine-day <u>trip</u>, they were <u>surprised</u> to hear a <u>loud sound</u> coming from behind a <u>big</u> tree. The leader <u>hurried ahead</u> to find himself <u>looking</u> into the <u>bright</u> eyes of an <u>angry</u> and <u>fierce</u> tiger with a <u>wide</u> mouth, <u>sharp</u> teeth, and a <u>hungry</u> look about it. With one quick <u>jump</u> and a <u>loud sound</u>, the tiger <u>ate</u> the leader. Deciding that the man was a <u>good bite</u>, the tiger <u>smelled</u> the air, looking for more people to <u>eat</u>. Following the <u>smell</u>, he <u>ran</u> straight toward the <u>scared people</u> to <u>go on with</u> his <u>meal</u>. Acting <u>quickly</u>, a man <u>got</u> a <u>gun</u> and <u>pointed</u> it at the tiger. He <u>pulled</u> the trigger, and there was a <u>big bang</u>! Smoke <u>was in</u> the air. When it <u>went away</u>, the <u>scared</u> people <u>looked at</u> the <u>place</u> where the tiger had been. They were <u>surprised</u> to see nothing there. All that <u>was left</u> of the tiger was a <u>yellow</u> and <u>brown</u> striped hammock <u>tied</u> between two trees. "Oh, dear," <u>said</u> the man. "What I was <u>aiming</u> for was a tiger-skin <u>carpet</u>!"

WORD LIST

ravenous	hanging	delicious
dense	rifle	grabbed
travelers	sped	feast
hostile	tremendous	cleared
peering	resounding	sighed
sniffed	frightened	area
remained	devoured	caravan
explosion	cavernous	forward
squeezed	razor-edged	golden
snarl	cinnamon	deafening
startled	trembling	pounce
glowing	aimed	amazed
safari	swiftly	filled
rushed	consume	scent
roar	continue	rug
morsel	scanned	huge
shooting	ferocious	

Name _____ Date _____

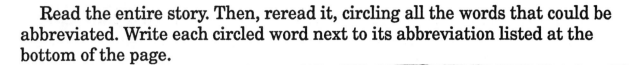

Read the entire story. Then, reread it, circling all the words that could be abbreviated. Write each circled word next to its abbreviation listed at the bottom of the page.

Mistress Evans, who lives in the Tower Apartment Building on Centennial Boulevard, fell down the stairs and broke her leg. Her neighbor, Mister Bradley, was nearby and immediately telephoned Doctor Tugwell at his office on West Main Street. Since it was Monday morning, September first, the office was closed and everyone was on holiday.

Thinking quickly, Mister Bradley dialed the number for Saint Andrews Hospital on Westchester Avenue and asked for the Emergency Department. He explained the situation to a nurse, who said, "Tell Mistress Evans that an ambulance from Hospital Helpers, Incorporated is leaving now to pick her up and bring her here."

Mistress Evans was relieved to know that help was on the way, but she was still very angry. She said, "It's the building superintendent's fault! If he had fixed that broken step three weeks ago when we reported it, none of this would have happened. I'm going to call my attorney!"

Just then, Captain Norton of Ships, International came up the stairs. "Avast there, you lubbers," he boomed, "you look like a ship stuck on a sandbar! What's the problem?"

Mister Bradley told Captain Norton what had happened, and Mistress Evans repeated her plans to contact her attorney. The captain nodded his head sympathetically and said, "Tell your attorney to contact the Sunshine Realty Company at 29 South Watley Court. They own this building."

Suddenly, three people in white uniforms carrying a stretcher over seven feet long entered the stairwell. Captain Norton exclaimed, "Right this way . . . right up here! Hurry—we've been waiting for at least an hour, and this lady's leg is as swollen as a gallon jug! Look lively there! You've wasted five minutes just staring! What you need is six months in the Navy to teach you to move!"

The ambulance attendants ran up the stairs, put Mistress Evans on the stretcher, and bundled her into the ambulance. As they drove away, Mister Bradley shook his head and said, "Poor Mistress Evans. It's too bad that she had to start the Fall with a fall!"

Abbreviations

ct. _____	supt. _____	Sept. _____	Mrs. _____
St. _____	1st _____	Bldg. _____	Dept. _____
ft _____	min _____	Blvd. _____	Capt. _____
mos. _____	Mon. _____	a.m. _____	Apt. _____
Mr. _____	wks. _____	Ave. _____	Dr. _____
W. _____	St. _____	Inc. _____	att. _____
co. _____	hr _____	gal. _____	S. _____

Name _____ Date _____

CONTRACTION FRACTIONS

You know that when you work with fractions in math, you must reduce them to the lowest common denominators. Contractions are similar to fractions in that they "reduce" two words into one smaller word. Work the Contraction Fractions below. Then put the answers to the Contraction Fractions into action by writing a short story titled "Mr. Jackson's Reaction" on a separate sheet of paper. Include and underline at least 10 contractions.

$\dfrac{do}{not}$ = _____ $\dfrac{I}{am}$ = _____ $\dfrac{we}{are}$ = _____

$\dfrac{he}{is}$ = _____ $\dfrac{should}{not}$ = _____ $\dfrac{you}{have}$ = _____

$\dfrac{would}{not}$ = _____ $\dfrac{it}{is}$ = _____ $\dfrac{they}{are}$ = _____

$\dfrac{she}{will}$ = _____ $\dfrac{are}{not}$ = _____ $\dfrac{there}{is}$ = _____

$\dfrac{was}{not}$ = _____ $\dfrac{you}{will}$ = _____ $\dfrac{can}{not}$ = _____

$\dfrac{you}{are}$ = _____ $\dfrac{will}{not}$ = _____ $\dfrac{has}{not}$ = _____

$\dfrac{were}{not}$ = _____ $\dfrac{I}{will}$ = _____ $\dfrac{does}{not}$ = _____

Name _____   Date _____

PLURAL DECISIONS

To solve the puzzle and find the hidden word, mark T (for True) or F (for False) beside each sentence below. If the sentence is true, shade in the puzzle spaces indicated. (For example, if sentence #1 is true, shade in all of the #1 spaces in the puzzle.) If the the sentence is false, do not shade in any of the spaces.

____ 1. To make the word **baby** mean more than one, change the **y** to **i** and add **es**.

____ 2. To make the word **fox** mean more than one, add **es**.

____ 3. To make the word **boy** mean more than one, change the **y** to **i** and add **es**.

____ 4. To make the word **knife** mean more than one, change the **fe** to **v** and add **es**.

____ 5. To make the work **girl** mean more than one, add **es**.

____ 6. To make the word **clock** mean more than one, change the **k** to **i** and add **es**.

____ 7. To make the word **flower** mean more than one, add **s**.

____ 8. To make the word **church** mean more than one, add **s**.

____ 9. To make the word **pencil** mean more than one, add **s**.

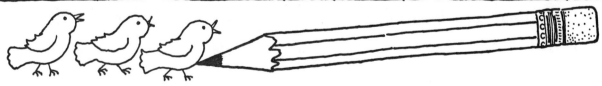

On a separate sheet of paper, write the plural form of each of the following words: monkey   bird   party   porch   tax   noun   life

Name _____   Date_____

©1994 by INCENTIVE PUBLICATIONS, Inc., Nashville, TN.

POSITIVELY POSSESSIVES

Read the following sentences to solve the puzzle and discover the hidden message. If a sentence has a word containing an apostrophe to show possession, shade in the spaces in the picture that have that sentence number. (For example, if sentence #1 contains a word with an apostrophe to show possession, shade in all the #1 spaces.)

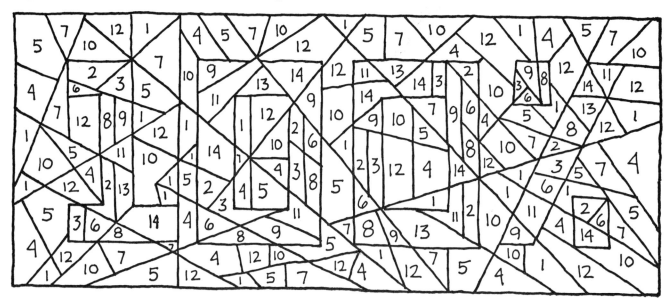

1. Matthew's day started off badly.

2. First, he couldn't find his shoes.

3. Then he remembered that he didn't do his homework.

4. His mother's car was broken, so he had to walk to school.

5. When he finally got to class, his teacher's question was, "Why are you so late?"

6. Matthew answered sadly, "I'm sorry, but everything just went wrong this morning."

7. Matthew started to do his work, but his pencil's point broke.

8. "I can't stand this much longer," thought Matthew.

9. "Never mind," whispered his friend April, "here's another one for you."

10. When test time came, Matthew's teacher handed out the papers.

11. Matthew groaned, "I'll never be able to answer all these questions!"

12. When he finished, he handed in his paper and watched the teacher's red pen move across his page.

13. "Good for you, Matthew," said his teacher at last, "you've made 100%!"

14. Matthew grinned and said, "Wow! Hasn't this day improved!"

Name _____ Date_____

— HETTIE HARNESSES HETERONYMS —

Help Hettie Heteronym harness the heteronyms that have been left out of this story. Use the heteronyms listed below to fill in the blanks and complete the story: record   live   read   tear

Hettie Heteronym had a marvelous new book to _____. It was a sequel to the one she had _____ last week. Last week's book had been about a _____ dog and a stuffed cat. In the story, the dog had gone to _____ with a new master, and the cat had been sent along to keep him company. The former owner had been sad to see the dog go, and could not resist shedding a _____ or two. When Hettie finished the book, she sympathized with the wear and _____ brought about by the dog's separation from his master.

Now Hettie was ready to begin the new book. She put her favorite _____ on the turntable and curled up on the sofa. She could hardly wait to find out what sort of adventure the author would _____ in this new book.

A heteronym is a word spelled like another word, but which is pronounced differently and has a different meaning.

On a separate sheet of paper, write a creative ending to the story using these or other heteronyms:

close   project   refuse   wind

Name _____   Date_____

THE MEANING OF MATH

Read each sentence below and fill in each blank with a word from the math vocabulary list. Use each word only once.

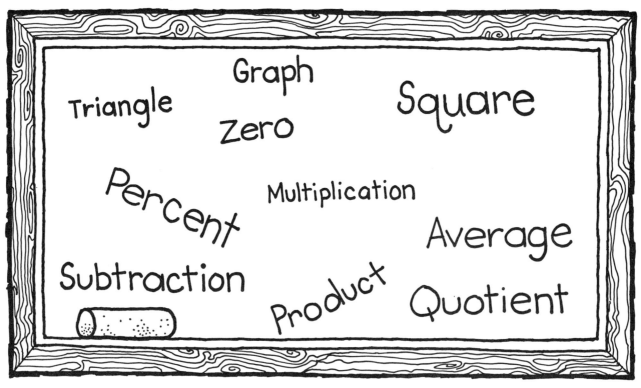

Triangle Graph Square Zero Percent Multiplication Average Subtraction Product Quotient

1. A _____ is a three-sided polygon.

2. If all of the members of your class are present, the attendance will be 100 _____ and perfect.

3. A drawing showing relationships between sets is known as a _____ .

4. _____ is an operation for computing repeated addition.

5. If you divide 63 by 9, the _____ would be 7.

6. _____ is the number of members in an empty set.

7. ☐ This is a _____ .

8. The sum of a set of numbers divided by the number of addends is known as the _____ .

9. When you multiply 9 times 9, 81 is the _____ .

10. When one addend and the sum are known, the operation used to find the missing addend is _____ .

Name _____ Date_____

HERE'S LOOKING AT YOU

Draw a picture of yourself here. You may make it realistic or cartoon-like. Think about the physical features that make you special, and try to represent them in your drawing.

Write five words that you think could be used to describe how you look. Look up each of the words in your dictionary (after you have written them, please!) to check their spellings and meanings. Then write the page number on which you found each of the words in the dictionary.

	Word	Page No.
1.	_____	_____
2.	_____	_____
3.	_____	_____
4.	_____	_____
5.	_____	_____

Now, write one word that you feel sums up the word picture you have painted of yourself. Write the word and its complete meaning from the dictionary on the lines below.

_____

_____

_____

_____

Does the word mean exactly what you thought it did? _____

On the lines below, write three words that describe your personality. Then look up the words in the dictionary to check their spellings and complete meanings. Beside each word, write the number of dictionary meanings given. You may find that your personality is more complex than you thought!

1. _____ 2. _____ 3. _____

Circle the word below that you think best sums up your personality.

complex   gregarious   dynamic

Look up that word in the dictionary and use the meaning to help you write a short paragraph (on a separate sheet of paper) to explain yourself to the world.

Name _____ Date _____

Find the first food listed in your dictionary. Write the name of the food and the page number on which you found it.

Food: _____ Page No.: _____

Find the last vegetable listed in your dictionary. Write that word and the words that appear above and below it in the dictionary in these blanks.

Food: _____ Page No.: _____

The following words are all ways to prepare meat. Look up the words in your dictionary and write the meaning for each in your own words.

Broil – _____

Sauté – _____

Fry – _____

Braise – _____

Sear – _____

Boil – _____

Bake – _____

Which of these methods would you use to cook a turkey? _____

In your own words, write a definition of the word "gourmet."

_____

_____

_____

_____

_____

On a separate sheet of paper design a menu for a gourmet meal you would like to have prepared for your next birthday. Look up any words you don't know how to spell.

Name _____ Date_____

DINER'S KNOW-HOW

People enjoy eating out. One recent report shows that one out of every three food dollars in the United States is spent on food eaten outside of the home.

Can you read a menu and tell what you will be receiving for your money? Use a reference book for help in completing this exercise.

1. To order "soup de jour," you would need to know _____.

2. How are "table d'hôte" and "à la carte" different?_____
_____
_____

3. Name four beverages you might order.
_____
_____

4. A "quiche" is _____.

5. "Stir-fried vegetables" are_____
_____

6. "Souffles" are made by _____
_____.

7. The difference between "boiled" and "broiled" is _____
_____
_____.

8. A tossed green salad is usually made from_____,
_____ and _____.

9. "Burger" is short for _____; "shake" is short for
_____, and "fries" are really _____.

10. At the end of every perfect meal, there's the "gratuity." What does this mean?_____

Name _____ Date_____

©1994 by Incentive Publications, Inc., Nashville, TN.

❖ FEELING FINDERS ❖

PURPOSE: Associating words with feelings

PREPARATION

1. Reproduce copies of the Feeling Finders worksheet on page 21.

2. Cut along the dotted lines to make fifteen word cards.

3. Place each set of cards in unsealed envelopes, and distribute to students.

4. Make available to students the Procedure directions below and a good collection of books appropriate for the students' reading interests portraying strong character and personality traits in a variety of settings.

PROCEDURE

1. Write your name and the date on the front of the envelope.

2. Read the word on each card, and try to remember a time when you felt like the word on the card. Think about the circumstances that caused you to feel that way.

3. Look through books on the reading table to find a sentence that shows a story character experiencing the same feeling.

4. Write the sentence, the name of the character, the title of the book, and the page number on the back of the word card. Here's an example:

5. Continue until you have completed all of the cards. Seal the envelope. On the front of the envelope write the date on which you completed the exercise.

6. Place the envelope in the box on the reading table to be opened at a given time when examples will be shared and discussed.

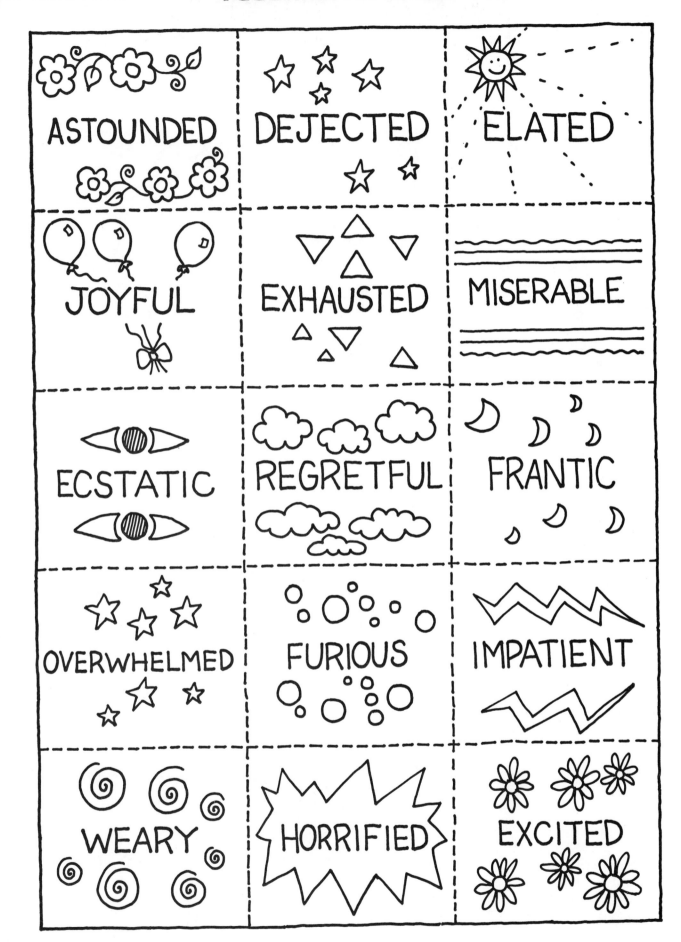

ASTOUNDED	DEJECTED	ELATED
JOYFUL	EXHAUSTED	MISERABLE
ECSTATIC	REGRETFUL	FRANTIC
OVERWHELMED	FURIOUS	IMPATIENT
WEARY	HORRIFIED	EXCITED

SHOW YOUR FEELINGS

Find and circle at least 35 words that express a mood or a feeling in the word-find puzzle below.

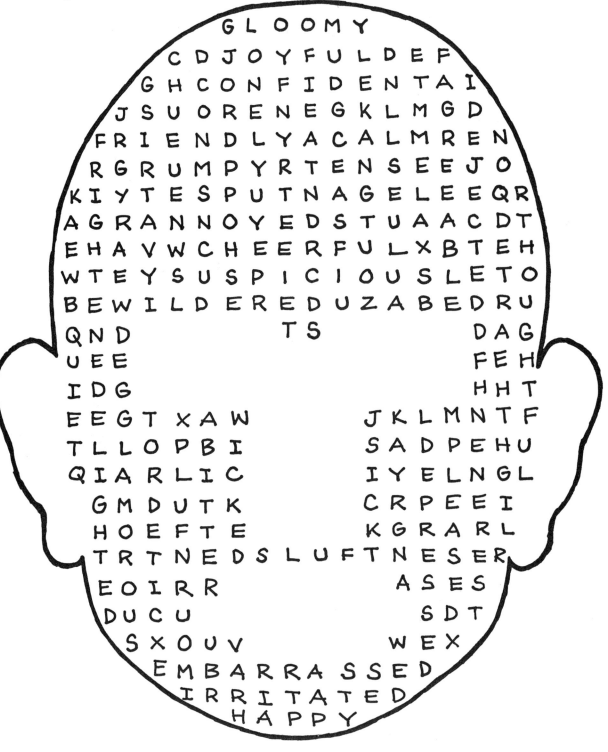

```
            G L O O M Y
          C D J O Y F U L D E F
        G H C O N F I D E N T A I
        J S U O R E N E G K L M G D
      F R I E N D L Y A C A L M R E N
      R G R U M P Y R T E N S E E J O
    K I Y T E S P U T N A G E L E E Q R
    A G R A N N O Y E D S T U A A C D T
    E H A V W C H E E R F U L X B T E H
    W T E Y S U S P I C I O U S L E T O
    B E W I L D E R E D U Z A B E D R U
    Q N D           T S           D A G
    U E E                         F E H
    I D G                         H H T
    E E G T X A W         J K L M N T F
    T L L O P B I         S A D P E H U
    Q I A R L I C         I Y E L N G L
    G M D U T K           C R P E E I
    H O E F T E           K G R A R L
    T R T N E D S L U F T N E S E R
    E O I R R                 A S E S
    D U C U                   S D T
    S X O U V             W E X
        E M B A R R A S S E D
        I R R I T A T E D
        H A P P Y
```

Add facial features, hair, and any other features you like to make the face express a feeling or a mood.

Name _____ Date_____

BIRDS OF A FEATHER DO WHAT?

Wait for me fellas!

ENGLISH

MATH

READING

. . . FLOCK TOGETHER!

In as few words as possible, write what you think each of these sayings means.

A fool and his money are soon parted. _____

_____

_____

All that glitters is not gold. _____

_____

_____

A little knowledge is a dangerous thing. _____

_____

_____

Don't count your chickens before they hatch. _____

_____

_____

Early to bed, early to rise, makes a man healthy, wealthy, and wise. _____

_____

_____

A bird in the hand is worth two in the bush. _____

_____

_____

Select one of the sayings above. Copy it on a separate sheet of paper, and illustrate it to make a poster for your classroom.

Name _____ Date _____

TIME ON THE LINE

A time line records important events over a given period of time.

Select a person whose life interests you and make a time line for that person. You may choose either a fictional character or a real person, but it must be a person whose life is written about in a book available to you. (At a later time, you may want to make a time line for a friend, your teacher, or even yourself!)

Read the material about the person's life and select eight important facts to record on a time line.

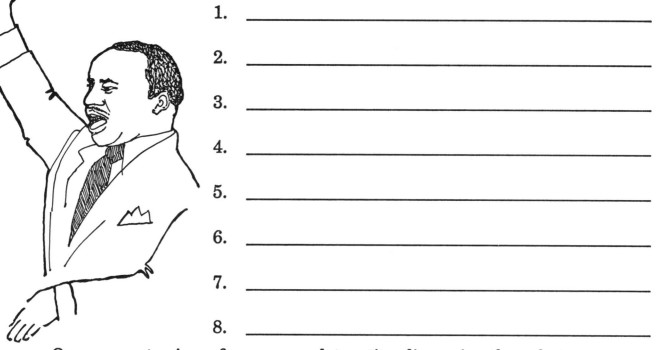

1. _____
2. _____
3. _____
4. _____
5. _____
6. _____
7. _____
8. _____

On a separate piece of paper, complete a time line using these facts.

EXAMPLE:

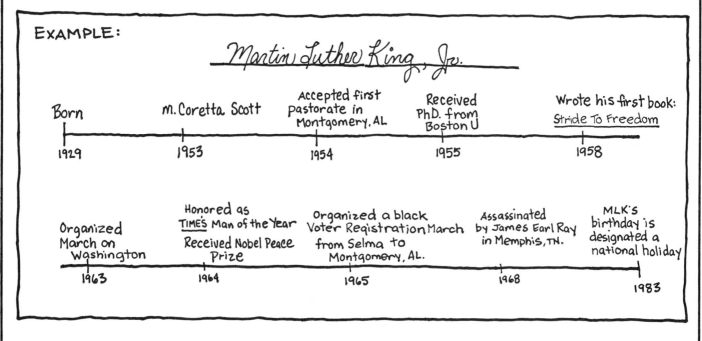

Martin Luther King, Jr.

Born	m. Coretta Scott	Accepted first pastorate in Montgomery, AL	Received PhD. from Boston U	Wrote his first book: Stride To Freedom
1929	1953	1954	1955	1958

Organized March on Washington	Honored as TIME'S Man of the Year / Received Nobel Peace Prize	Organized a black Voter Registration March from Selma to Montgomery, AL.	Assassinated by James Earl Ray in Memphis, TN.	MLK'S birthday is designated a national holiday
1963	1964	1965	1968	1983

Name _____   Date _____

❖ FRONT PAGE REVIEW ❖

PURPOSE: Finding answers to specific questions

PREPARATION

1. Assemble enough newspapers for each student to have one.

2. Reproduce and distribute the Front Page Review worksheet (page 26), and provide a pencil for each student.

PROCEDURE

1. Follow the directions on the Front Page Review worksheet (page 26).

FOLLOW-UP ACTIVITY DIRECTIONS

1. Read and discuss student worksheets.

2. Write vital information for a front page article on the chalkboard. Include information based on the "5 W and How" reporter's questions (What? Where? When? Who? Why? How?).
   Add a few extraneous bits of information (e.g., witnesses, quotes, brief background information, etc.).

3. Direct students to write the article themselves, presenting information as clearly and as concisely as possible.

4. Direct students to write headlines for their articles.

5. Share and compare the articles.

FRONT PAGE REVIEW

Select an article from the front page of the newspaper.

1. Write the complete headline.

   _____

2. Read the entire article carefully.

3. Circle six key words in the article. Write them here.

   _____   _____   _____

   _____   _____   _____

4. Circle three key phrases. Write them here.

   _____

   _____

   _____

5. Who is featured in the article? _____

6. What is the article about? _____

   _____

7. Where did the event take place? _____

   _____

8. Circle the one sentence that gives the main idea or carries the "punch
   line" of the article. Write the sentence. _____

   _____

   _____

9. Do you think the article tells everything it should? _____
   Why?_____

   _____

10. Do you think the headline tells what the article is really about, or is it
    misleading?_____ Why? _____

    _____

11. Write a different headline for the article. _____

    _____

Name _____   Date_____

©1994 by Incentive Publications, Inc., Nashville, TN.

❖ FUNNEL YOUR READING ❖

PURPOSE: Using key words, phrases, and topic sentences to understand main ideas

PREPARATION

1. Assign to students reading selections in content areas, and provide pencils and copies of the Reading Funnel worksheet (page 28) for each student.

2. Assemble content materials to be read, and give any needed pre-reading directions (such as new words, references to future use of material, etc.).

PROCEDURE

1. Read the assigned material carefully.

2. Reread and copy from the article any key words, key phrases, and one main topic sentence in the proper spaces on the Reading Funnel worksheet.

3. Review the words, phrases, and topic sentences. Use all three elements to help you write the main idea of the selection.

4. Write the name of the book and the page number at the bottom of the "funnel" for easy reference.

Note: After you have used this form enough to become familiar with it, you can adapt it to index cards for easier use when preparing reports or projects requiring more than one source of material.

READING FUNNEL WORKSHEET

Topic:_____

Key Words: _____

_____

_____

   Key Phrases:_____

   _____

   _____

      Topic Sentence or Sentences: _____

      _____

      _____

      _____

         Main Ideas:_____

         _____

         _____

         _____

         _____

         _____

         _____

         _____

         _____

            Book: _____

            _____

            _____

            Page # _____

Name _____   Date_____

PEERING AT PARAGRAPHS

Read the following paragraphs, and underline the topic sentence in each.

Marion was sitting on the front steps, enjoying the sun on her face. She looked up and down the street. Trees and bushes were beginning to turn green, and some early flowers were in bloom. Patches of grass were showing on the brown lawns. Down the block, some kids were playing baseball. Marion smiled. Spring had finally arrived.

Raindrops began to patter on the roof. The wind grew strong and began to roar about the house. Thunder crashed and boomed, and lightning sparkled and flashed its way across the sky. Gathering clouds blotted out the daylight, and the rain came down hard and thick. The storm we had been waiting for all day finally broke.

"I've looked everywhere for that book!" thought Tony. "I remember bringing it home and putting it on the counter. Then I took it into my bedroom to read after supper. I've looked on the counter, and it isn't there. I've searched the bedroom, and it isn't there. What could have happened to it?"

It was time for the party to begin. All the decorations were up; balloons and streamers were everywhere. The long table had flowers in the center and was loaded with food. A full punch bowl sat at one end of the table, and a giant cake filled the other. A big stack of beautifully wrapped presents was waiting, ready to be opened.

Choose any of the paragraphs above. On a separate sheet of paper write two more paragraphs to go with it. Your first paragraph must come before the chosen paragraph, and your second paragraph must follow it.

Name _____ Date_____

©1994 by Incentive Publications, Inc., Nashville, TN.

DETAIL DEDUCTION

Learning to read for details is an important skill for good readers to acquire. Practice using this skill by finding, circling, and labeling the parts of the sentences below that tell "who," "what," "where," "when," "why," and "how."

Give yourself a reasonable time limit, and show off your "Detail Deduction" skills by finishing this sheet in the allotted amount of time.

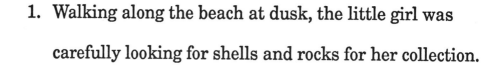

Example:

who	what	where	how
Jennifer	worked to finish her chores	in the garden	quickly

why	when
so that she could catch the train	before noon.

1. Walking along the beach at dusk, the little girl was carefully looking for shells and rocks for her collection.

2. Many people work very hard in hotels in order to gain experience while they are in management school.

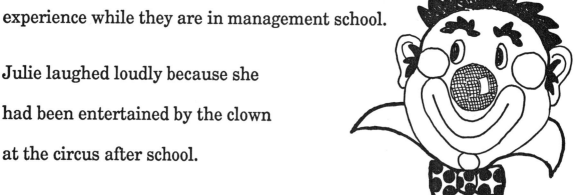

3. Julie laughed loudly because she had been entertained by the clown at the circus after school.

4. Danny, the dog, barked wildly outside the gate to signal the stranger's midnight arrival.

5. The family bravely searched the forest all day long because of their concern for the lost child.

6. Mrs. Andrews smiled happily as she sat on the porch in the morning sun to read the long letter from her friend.

Name _____ Date_____

©1994 by Incentive Publications, Inc., Nashville, TN.

ANALOGIES ON DEPOSIT

Find a word in the safe that completes each sentence. Use each word only once.

1. Thorn is to rose as barnacle is to _____.

2. Tine is to fork as blade is to _____.

3. Petal is to flower as leaf is to _____.

4. Feather is to bird as fin is to
   _____.

5. Museum is to art as bank is to
   _____.

6. Necklace is to neck as ring is to
   _____.

7. Dust is to the desert as sand is
   to the _____.

8. Tooth is to a comb as rung is to
   a _____.

9. Shoe is to foot as glove is to
   _____.

10. Fur is to a cat as grass is to a
    _____.

11. A driver is to a bus as a pilot is
    to an _____.

BLACK Tree Meadow Knife Hand EARTH MONEY Box Carpenter LADDER FINGER Airplane Dog Seashore SHELL Fish

12. A spoon is to a cook as a hammer is to a _____.

13. Day is to night as white is to _____.

14. A planet is to the sun as our moon is to the _____.

15. A roof is to a house as a top is to a _____.

16. A kitten is to a cat as a puppy is to a _____.

Name _____ Date_____

❖ SPECIAL NEWS WATCH ❖

PURPOSE: Understanding/summarizing main ideas

PREPARATION

1. Reproduce copies of the Special News Watch worksheet (page 33).

PROCEDURE

1. Read each bulletin carefully.

2. Underline once the information that you feel should be included in a special television news flash.

3. Underline twice the most important sentence.

4. Circle the unnecessary sentences and phrases.

5. Rewrite the bulletin using as few words as possible.

SPECIAL NEWS WATCH

NEWS BULLETIN

Just after noon today, three prisoners escaped from the State Prison located at 4609 Cumberland Circle East. These three prisoners are thought to be armed and are considered very dangerous. At the time of their escape, they were wearing olive green prison uniforms. They escaped by hooking bed sheets together to make a rope to scale the prison wall. All three were serving 99-year sentences for murder and armed robbery. The prisoners are thought to be on foot, still together, and seeking a way to leave the state. Police helicopters joined in the search about two hours after the escape. All area residents are asked to be on the alert for these escaped prisoners and to call local police at this number, 555-1234, if they have any reason to think they have spotted these people.

· · ·NEWS BULLETIN· · · ·

────WEATHER BULLETIN────

WEATHER BULLETIN

At 6:00 P.M. today, the United States Weather Bureau posted a special watch for the following states: Tennessee, Georgia, Florida, Virginia, North Carolina, South Carolina, Alabama, New York, and parts of Pennsylvania and Delaware. Severe winds, heavy rainfall, and electrical storms are predicted within the next twenty-four hours. As clouds build up and storm signals continue to develop off the East Coast, all area residents are advised to be alert for further news of storm warnings, flooding, and a posted tornado watch. This storm appears to be similar in nature to last week's storm in the same area, and is expected to be equally severe.

Name _____ Date _____

©1994 by Incentive Publications, Inc., Nashville, TN.

FISHY FACTS FILMSTRIPS

Many movies and filmstrips were first written in book form. These books were made into films for a variety of reasons, one of which is that many people remember what they see better than what they read.

Locate and read through several different sources of information about fish. Select at least eight major facts that you have learned from your reading, and write these in complete sentences on the lines below.

1. _____
2. _____
3. _____
4. _____
5. _____
6. _____
7. _____
8. _____
9. _____
10. _____

Use the Fishy Facts Filmstrip worksheet (page 35) to produce your own filmstrip.

1. In the first rectangle, write a title for your filmstrip. In the last rectangle, write "The End."

2. List one "Fishy Fact" in each rectangle. Write them in any style you choose, and add illustrations to each frame that will help the viewer understand what you have written.

3. Show your filmstrip to classmates, and keep a log of their comments about your work.

Name _____   Date _____

FISHY FACTS FILMSTRIPS

Name _____   Date_____

❖ ABSOLUTELY ACCURATE ANSWERS ❖

PURPOSE: Reading to verify answers

PREPARATION

1. Select a chapter or unit from a content area textbook (science, social studies, etc.).

2. Reproduce a copy of the Absolutely Accurate Answers worksheet (page 37) for each student.

PROCEDURE

1. Distribute the worksheets to the students.

2. Ask students to read the selection and to write seven key words or phrases from the material in the spaces provided on the worksheet. Have students follow the directions for completion.

3. After answers have been checked and scores determined, lead a follow-up discussion on the different types of reading skills needed for studying content-area materials.

- INFERENCE
- SKIMMING
- FINDING MAIN IDEAS
- READING TO VERIFY ANSWERS
- READING FOR DETAILS

ABSOLUTELY ACCURATE ANSWERS

Write seven key words or phrases from the material you have just read. Then, without looking at your book, write the best definition you can for each of the words or phrases.

1. _____
_____

2. _____
_____

3. _____
_____

4. _____
_____

5. _____
_____

6. _____
_____

7. _____
_____

Now, reread the material carefully to check your answers. Be completely honest and determine your score. Give yourself:

10 points for each Absolutely Accurate answer;
5 points for Almost Accurate answers
0 points for Inaccurate answers.

WORD	ABSOLUTELY ACCURATE	ALMOST ACCURATE	INACCURATE	POINTS
1.				
2.				
3.				
4.				
5.				
6.				
7.				TOTAL____

Name _____ Date_____

❖ WHAT WILL HAPPEN? ❖

PURPOSE: Drawing conclusions

PREPARATION

1. Gather the following materials:
   - fish bowl or other container
   - paper squares or index cards
   - felt-tipped pens

2. On each of the index cards, write an open-ended situation that would be of interest to the students.

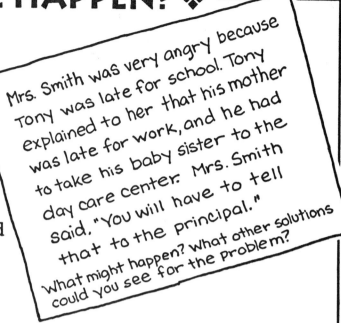

Mrs. Smith was very angry because Tony was late for school. Tony explained to her that his mother was late for work, and he had to take his baby sister to the day care center. Mrs. Smith said, "You will have to tell that to the principal."

What might happen? What other solutions could you see for the problem?

The factory workers asked for an extra coffee break because there was no air conditioning on the assembly line. The foreman said they were turning out less work already because of the hot weather, and the company could not afford another break.

What might happen next?

Betty and Sue had been friends for a long time. Their quarrel concerned a party to which Betty was invited and Sue was not. Sue felt that Betty should not go to the party, but Betty said that it had nothing to do with friendship and that she planned to go to the party.

Who is right?

PROCEDURE

1. Several students may play this game, or it may be used in a small reading group.

2. Sit in a circle and pass the bowl to each participant.

3. Each player reaches into the bowl, draws one card, reads the card chosen to the group, and explains what he or she thinks would be a logical conclusion to the situation.

4. The other players discuss the conclusion to determine if it is "logical," and if there could be other logical conclusions. (Discussion and exchange of ideas are important features of this game.)

AESOP'S WORKSHOP

Aesop was a slave in Greece more than two thousand years ago. We remember him for the fables he wrote and the lessons that they teach.

Read each of the following summaries of some of Aesop's fables and figure out what you think is the lesson each teaches. Write it on the line below the story.

THE CAT AND THE MICE

Once there were some mice who were harassed by a cat. They held a meeting to decide what to do about it. One mouse stood up and said, "Since the cat moves so quietly, we can't hear it coming. If it had a bell tied around its neck, we would hear it ringing and could run to safety before it could catch us."

The other mice were delighted by this clever plan until one old mouse stood up and said, "Yes, it's a good plan. But who is going to put the bell on the cat?"

THE BOY AND THE WOLF

There was a young boy who tended sheep in a village. Since he often found his job boring, he would create some excitement by running to the village and yelling "Wolf! Wolf!" as loudly as he could. All the villagers would come running with tools and clubs to help him, only to find that he had played a trick on them.

The boy thought this was funny, and did it several times. But one day, a real wolf actually did come out of the forest. This time, when the boy ran to the village calling, "Wolf!" no one came to help him. The wolf ate all the sheep he wanted!

THE GRASSHOPPER AND THE ANT

It was winter, and the grasshopper was cold and hungry. He saw an ant eating some grains that had been stored during the summer, so he asked the ant to share his food.

"Didn't you store up some food last summer for the winter?" asked the ant.

"No," replied the grasshopper, "I was too busy singing then."

"Too bad," said the ant. "Since you sang all summer, you can just dance all winter!"

Choose one of the fables, and rewrite it with a modern setting.

Name _____ Date _____

PREDICTION PUZZLES

Each story starter below presents a situation with several possible outcomes. Read the story beginnings, and copy them onto another sheet of paper. Then complete them by writing what you think will happen in each case.

Bertha and Alfred had been walking in the woods all afternoon. When the sun began to set, they decided to head home. Alfred led the way down a path that curved and suddenly ended in front of a tall, wire fence.

"Hmm," said Alfred uncertainly. "I was sure this was the right path to take, but I don't remember this fence.

"Oh, no," Bertha sighed, "don't tell me we're lost! And it's getting dark, too. What will we do?"

The kitty huddled against the building, trying to get out of the rain. It was cold and wet, and tired of being lost. The kitty meowed sadly. How it wished that it could go to a warm, dry home.

Suddenly, the kitty saw a shadow and heard a person coming toward it.

Terry stretched and yawned as he woke up, wondering why he felt so uncomfortable. He opened his eyes and saw that his lamp was still on. Then he realized that he had slept in his clothes.

"Wow!" Terry groaned. "I must have fallen asleep last night when I was studying for my test! Now it's time to go to school, and I'm not ready! What am I going to do?"

"Be quiet," called Stanley as he closed the classroom door and hurried back to his seat. "She's coming down the hall now. Everybody get ready for the big surprise!"

Ms. Gregory walked in and sat down at her desk. "Good morning, class," she smiled. "How is everyone today?"

"Good morning, Ms. Gregory," replied the students. Then they called out, "Surprise! Happy Birthday! We brought you a cake! Surprise!!"

Name _____

Date _____

THE RIGHT THING TO DO

Read the following paragraphs and write what you feel would be the best way to handle each situation. Use an additional sheet of paper if you need more space to write.

Craig had earned enough money from his dog-walking service to treat his friend Doug to the movies. He had invited Doug to go with him, and they were to meet at the theater at 1:30. At 12:00, Craig realized that if he paid Doug's way into the movie, there would not be enough money to buy popcorn and a drink for himself.

What do you think Craig should do? Why?

_____

_____

_____

Suzanne was having a very difficult time answering the questions on the history test. She hadn't studied enough and was wishing that she could wave her pencil over her paper and make the correct words appear. Just then, she noticed that Greg was sneaking a look at his history book to find the answers.

What do you think Suzanne should do, and why?

_____

_____

_____

Barbara's family had just moved to town, and Barbara had not met any kids her age. One day, Ted saw Barbara standing by herself and went over to meet her. They introduced themselves, and Barbara asked Ted to go roller skating with her. Just as they started to leave, Frank, Ted's best friend, walked up and wanted Ted to go fishing with him instead.

What do you think Ted should do, and why?

_____

_____

_____

_____

Name _____   Date_____

IDENTIFY THE IRRELEVANTS

Draw a line through the sentence in each paragraph that does not belong.

Yesterday I went to the library to find a book of fairy tales. I looked through the shelves and found one by Jakob and Wilhelm Grimm. There was another one by Hans Christian Andersen and one called *The Blue Book of Fairy Tales*. My mother said we were going to have hamburgers for dinner. I checked out the book of fairy tales by Hans Christian Andersen.

Richard couldn't believe where he was when he looked out of the window on the 25th of July. Snow was falling, covering the trees and flowers. Richard's sister Cheryl dropped her doll and began to cry. Richard watched the snowstorm in amazement. He wondered if he had somehow managed to sleep through the summer, so he checked the calendar. But it was still July. As he went back to the window, he shook his head in confusion and thought to himself, "I didn't know it could snow in July!"

Percival Prendergrast turned thirteen years old today. His mother and father gave him a new bike. His sister baked a cake for him. Percival's favorite color is green. At school, his friends wished him a happy birthday. His grandmother took him to see a movie. Percival had such a good time on his birthday that he decided to celebrate this same way every year.

My first swimming lesson was a real disaster! I was late to class because I wasted so much time in the dressing room. Then I got lost in the showers and couldn't find the pool. When I finally got there, I ran across to stand by my best friend, and the lifeguard blew the whistle at me to tell me not to run. I don't know how to whistle. When we were supposed to step carefully into the water, I slipped and fell in with a big splash. Then I tried to blow air out through my nose, but I choked. The teacher had to rescue me. After that, I just sat on the side and watched for the rest of the lesson.

Name _____   Date _____

❖ ARE YOU SURE ABOUT THAT? ❖

PURPOSE: Distinguishing between fact and opinion

PREPARATION

1. Reproduce copies of the Opinionated Statements worksheet (page 44).

PROCEDURE

1. Distribute copies of the Opinionated Statements worksheet (page 44).

2. Ask students to review the worksheets. Lead a class discussion to set the scene for individual writing.

3. After worksheets are completed, ask students to work in small groups composed of those who selected common topics.

4. After group discussion, each group should prepare a means of disproving the statement to the class. (This might be in the form of creative dramatics, panel discussion, written reports, cartoon series, or any other presentation.) The emphasis here should be on originality and teamwork.

VARIATIONS

1. Ask students to work in groups to make lists of other "Opinionated Statements."

2. Assign the worksheet as homework, and ask students to discuss it with their families and prepare the three-paragraph paper as a project representative of family thinking.

3. Ask each student to bring in one newspaper or magazine article in which the author's authority is in question. Mount all of the articles on a bulletin board or chart to use in a learning center or skills lab setting.

OPINIONATED STATEMENTS

Sometimes it's hard to tell the difference between a fact and an opinion. This is especially dangerous when a little bit of factual information is used as the basis for much discussion and writing.

Good readers need to learn to question the source of written material and the authority of the author in order to determine if the information really is factual.

Select one of the statements below, and (on a separate sheet of paper) write three paragraphs to disprove it. Write one paragraph telling why the statement is not true, and one paragraph telling how you think it may have started as an opinion and become accepted by some people as fact. In the third paragraph, discuss the possible personal consequences of accepting the statement as factual.

Use dictionaries, encyclopedias, or other reference materials if you need them.

1. All Eskimos live in igloos.
2. All soldiers are strong and brave.
3. San Francisco is sliding into the ocean.
4. Actors lead unhappy lives.
5. Flowers have sweet scents.
6. Dog owners are kind people.
7. Big business executives are not concerned about individual employees.

Name _____ Date _____

Distinguishing facts from opinions is not always easy. This is especially true in advertising. A producer thinks that his product is a good one and wants you to buy it, so the product is described in terms that will convince you that you need it.

Read the magazine ad below. Underline the facts in red and the opinions in blue. Be careful—sometimes they are mixed together in the same sentence!

PENCIL PACKERS, INC. presents . . .   · ADVERTISEMENT ·

. . . the *BEST* and most *MARVELOUS* PENCIL SHARPENER to ever appear on the market!!!

This powerful new pencil sharpener needs no plugs, no cords, no electrical outlets. It is battery-powered, and we think it will run for at least 3 years on its original units. Constructed with solid, top-quality aluminum blades, this machine will give your pencils sharper, cleaner, finer points than any produced by our competitors. There's no waiting, no messy dust or pencil shavings, no energy output on your part! Simply drop your pencil into the machine, and watch it roll out with the best point a pencil could have . . .

FAST, FAST, FAST!!!!!
You need this wonderful, work-saving tool—
. . . *at home*   . . . *at the office*   . . . *at school*
. . . *ANYWHERE you need a pencil!*

So hurry to your local *PENCIL PACKERS* dealer, and buy this remarkable sharpener at the special introductory bargain price of only $9.95. Supplies are limited, so don't delay!!
Get . . . The Point?

Remember . . .
at *PENCIL PACKERS, INC.*,
serving YOU is a *POINT* of PRIDE!

Rewrite this ad using only the facts. Then write a short paragraph explaining which opinions in the original ad interested you, and tell why.

Name _____ Date_____

MOOD MINDED

Below are several story excerpts in which the author's purpose was to create a certain mood or feeling. Read each one carefully, and identify its mood or feeling by matching each excerpt with a picture that expresses the same mood. Draw an arrow from the excerpt to the picture.

Then reread each story, and underline the key words that helped you understand the mood of the story.
(Excerpt A is done for you.)

A. The house stood <u>still</u> and <u>gaunt</u>—a <u>stark</u> silhouette against the <u>dull gray</u> sky, framed only by two <u>spindly</u> pines and a <u>lone, wind-whipped</u> Joshua tree.

B. A cozy cottage, with its happy, shining windows, was tucked snugly away in the protective custody of a maternal cluster of spreading maples.

C. The clouds above, lit silver by a full moon, shaded the shimmering beauty of the crystal-like waters below.

D. Jessica awoke, instantly alert and full of spirit. She climbed quickly from her bunk with a nimble animation that resembled the early-morning activities of the jays and squirrels outside her window. She was exuberantly delighted to be alive.

Name _____

Date _____

I'D RATHER SEE ONE THAN BE ONE!

Read the following paragraph carefully. Then (not before, please) read and follow the directions given.

The hippodoraffe is native to cool, dry climates, is a vegetarian, and is often spotted near tall fruit or berry-producing trees or shrubs. All evidence indicates that its extra-long neck and large stomach pouch make it possible for a hippodoraffe to store and maintain up to a week's supply of food and water in its own body. This enables the animal to use its long legs and big feet to take giant strides, run fast, and cover many miles in any given day. For this reason, a hippodoraffe is seldom victim to hunters or other enemies, and usually enjoys a long and healthy life. Hippodoraffes are reported to be strong and cunning and yet very gentle and cooperative. This evidence, as is all other data about the hippodoraffe's lifestyle and characteristics, is poorly documented due to the limited number of hippodoraffes available for observation. Scientists are continually on the lookout for a way to secure one or more pairs to place in captivity for observation.

Draw a picture of the hippodoraffe in its natural environment. Color your picture.

Reread the paragraph, and underline three sentences that caused you to visualize the hippodoraffe as you did.

Name _____ Date_____

❖ DISCONCERTING DICTIONARIES ❖

PURPOSE: Using the dictionary/interpreting symbols and keys

PREPARATION

1. Provide assorted colors of construction paper and felt-tipped pens for student use. Have several dictionaries on hand for students to use as references.

2. Write the directions below on a card, and place it with the other materials in a free-choice interest center.

PROCEDURE

1. Create 20 nonsense words to go into a "No-Such-Word" Dictionary, and decide what part of speech each word is. Browse through a dictionary to see how information such as plurals and endings is shown, and use that format as a guide to show all of the "technical" information you have created for each of your words.

2. Write 4 or 5 words (in alphabetical order, of course) with the accompanying technical information (phonetic symbols and keys) on each sheet of construction paper. Leave room to add definitions and illustrations later. Make an attractive cover, sign your name as "1st Author," and clip your pages together.

3. Exchange your "No-Such-Word Dictionary" for one written by a classmate. Read and think about his or her words. Then create a definition for each word, and write a sentence for each that shows your interpretation of the meaning you have assigned to it.

4. Sign your name as "2nd Author," and discuss both completed "No-Such-Word Dictionaries" with your co-author.

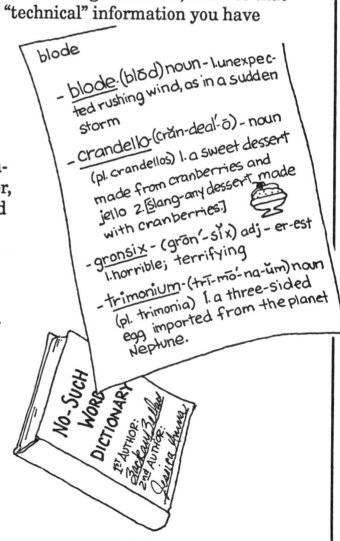

blode

- blode (blōd) noun - 1. unexpected rushing wind, as in a sudden storm

- crandello (crăn-deal'-ō) - noun (pl. crandellos) 1. a sweet dessert made from cranberries and jello 2. [Slang-any dessert made with cranberries.]

- gronsix - (grōn'-sĭx) adj - er-est 1. horrible; terrifying

- trimonium (trī-mō'-na-ŭm) noun (pl. trimonia) 1. a three-sided egg imported from the planet Neptune.

NO-SUCH WORD DICTIONARY
1ST AUTHOR:
2ND AUTHOR:

❖ QUESTIONS TO ANSWER ❖

PURPOSE: Using reference materials to find answers to specific questions

PREPARATION

1. Provide the following materials for the students:
   - question mark cards
   - box
   - atlas, encyclopedia, almanac, dictionary, thesaurus, *Guinness Book of World Records,* etc.
   - pencils or pens
   - paper

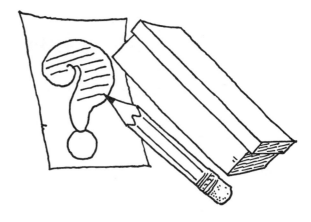

2. Use this pattern or one of your own to make question marks.

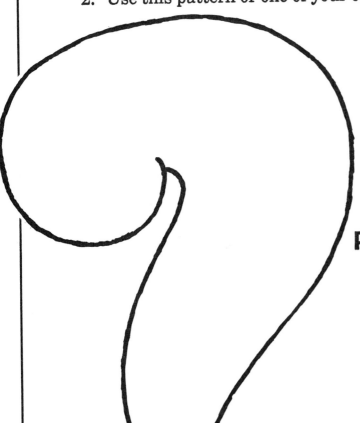

3. Print one of the statements or questions from page 50 (or use some of your own) on the front of each question mark. Print a number on the back.

4. Print the following directions on the top of the flat box, and place the question marks in the box for student use.

PROCEDURE

1. Select a question mark from the box. Read it carefully, and decide which reference book to use to find the best answer in the shortest amount of time.

2. When you have located the information, write the number from the back of the question mark on your paper, the reference book used, the page number, and the time it took you to locate the information.

3. Finish as many of the question mark questions as you can in the amount of time assigned.

QUESTIONS TO ANSWER

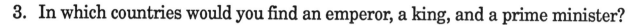

1. What is the difference between a souffle and an omelet?

2. Name six words that mean the same thing as "desert country."

3. In which countries would you find an emperor, a king, and a prime minister?

4. What is a polygraph?

5. What is the most heavily populated country in the world?

6. Where and when was the first airplane flown?

7. Name three sources to use to locate information about film-making.

8. What is a palindrome, and in what subjects in school would you need this definition?

9. Who was Copernicus, and what were his contributions to mankind?

10. What is the world land speed record?

11. What was Harriet Tubman known for?

12. Who compiled the first dictionary, and how long did it take?

13. Who was Alfred Nobel?

14. Who was the first female astronaut?

Name _____ Date _____

©1994 by Incentive Publications, Inc., Nashville, TN.

RELEVANT REFERENCES

Work the crossword puzzle below to show off your knowledge of sources that are used to locate information.

Where would you look to:

ACROSS

2. Check the day of the month?
5. Find a phone number?
9. Locate a library book?
10. Determine the distance between two cities?
11. Find information about the life and habits of elephants?

DOWN

1. Get ideas about fashion and/or home decorating?
3. Find the time of a favorite TV program and local advertising?
4. Find how many teaspoons equal one cup?
5. Find synonyms for a word?
6. Find the definition of a word?
7. Find the cost of a bicycle?
8. Learn where the world's deserts are located?

Name _____ Date_____

❖ TOWERING THESAURUS ❖

PURPOSE: Using the thesaurus

PREPARATION

1. Print appropriate category words on each shape on the Towering Thesaurus worksheet (page 53).

2. Reproduce the Towering Thesaurus worksheet (page 53).

3. Provide a thesaurus and the following Procedure directions for each participating student.

PROCEDURE

1. Use a thesaurus to find words associated with each category word given. Write the words you find in the appropriate blocks. (At least ten words must be listed in a shape before it may be used as a building block.)

2. When all of the shapes have been filled, cut them out and paste them onto another sheet of paper to build your own Thesaurus Tower.

3. Use your imagination to decorate and add interest to the completed tower.

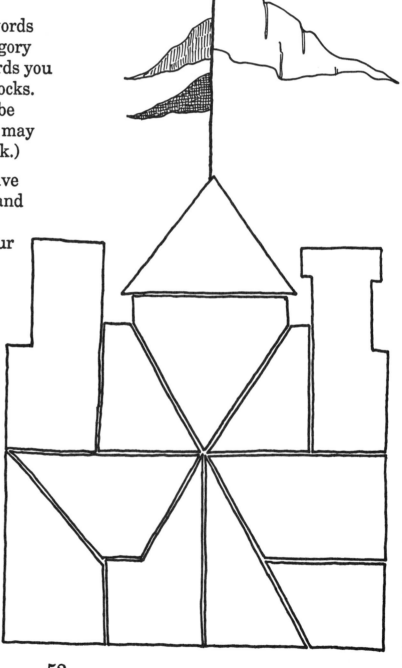

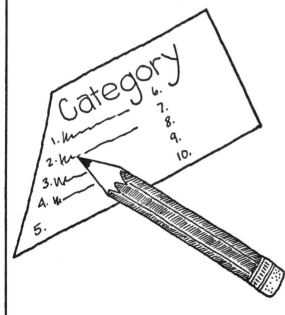

❖ HIGH-FLYING FLAGS ❖

PURPOSE: Using the encyclopedia

PREPARATION

1. Lead a group discussion of the encyclopedia and its uses. Ask students to identify the volume to use to locate information related to various topics, emphasizing that information can be found in more than one volume, but that there is usually one which has the most comprehensive coverage. This volume, then, is the primary source of information on the topic.

2. Provide encyclopedias and copies of the High-Flying Flags worksheet (page 55).

PROCEDURE

1. Complete the High-Flying Flags worksheet (page 55).

FOLLOW-UP ACTIVITY

1. Divide the class into small groups to research countries represented by the flags.

2. Each group selects or is assigned a different country and uses the encyclopedia to learn as much as possible about the geography, history, customs, industry, and social life of the country and its people.

3. At an appointed time, the groups will share their findings through any creative means they choose. Some suggestions are a panel discussion, mural, puppet or stage play, diorama, or scrapbook.

HIGH-FLYING FLAGS

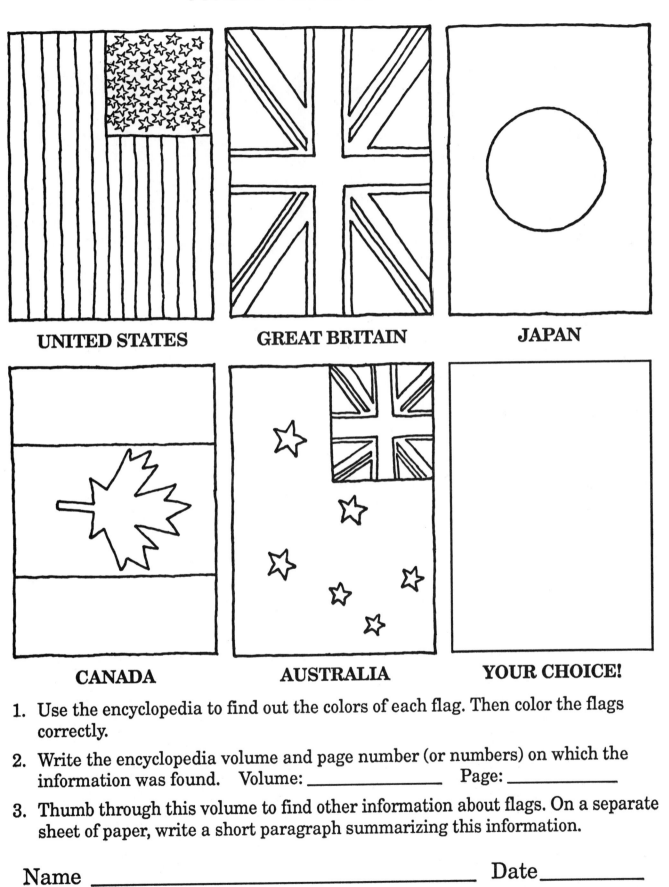

UNITED STATES **GREAT BRITAIN** **JAPAN**

CANADA **AUSTRALIA** **YOUR CHOICE!**

1. Use the encyclopedia to find out the colors of each flag. Then color the flags correctly.

2. Write the encyclopedia volume and page number (or numbers) on which the information was found. Volume: _____ Page: _____

3. Thumb through this volume to find other information about flags. On a separate sheet of paper, write a short paragraph summarizing this information.

Name _____ Date _____

CARD CATALOG COGITATION

The card catalog in every library has cards listing each book three ways: by subject, title, and author. If you know any of these 3 facts about a book, you can find a listing for it in the card catalog.

To reveal the hidden message in the puzzle on page 57, read each of the following statements. If the statement is true, mark a "T" beside the statement and shade in the corresponding number blocks in the picture. If the statement is false, mark an "F" beside the statement and leave the corresponding blocks unshaded.

_____ 1. If you wanted to read all of the "Just So" stories by Rudyard Kipling, you would first look in the card catalog for an author card with his name.

_____ 2. If you wanted to find out about the history of the United Nations, you would first look for a title card.

_____ 3. If you wanted to write an article about the world hunger crisis, you would first look for a subject card.

_____ 4. If you wanted to know who wrote *Mary Poppins,* you would look first for an author card.

_____ 5. If you wanted to make a list of all the books written by Charles Dickens, you would look first for a title card.

_____ 6. If you wanted to find a copy of *Spoon River Anthology,* you would first look for a title card.

_____ 7. If you wanted to read some of Eldridge Cleaver's writing, you would look first for a subject card.

_____ 8. If you wanted to know who wrote *Bambi,* you would look first for a title card.

_____ 9. If you remembered that Nikki Giovanni wrote a book of poetry that you wanted to read, but you couldn't remember the title of it, you would look first for an author card.

_____ 10. If you wanted to find J.R.R. Tolkein's book about hobbits, you would first find the title card.

_____ 11. If you wanted to browse through a collection of fairy tales by Jakob and Wilhelm Grimm, you would first look for an author card.

_____ 12. If you wanted to read Kenneth Grahame's book about the wild animals living along the river bank, you would first look for a title card.

_____ 13. If you wanted to find out more about scouting, you would first look for a title card.

Name _____ Date _____

❖ WORD ROUND-UP ❖

PURPOSE: Using newspapers and magazines

PREPARATION

1. Use weekly classroom newspapers and magazines to teach or reinforce word attack or vocabulary skills. Provide a copy of the paper or magazine, along with paper and pencils or pens, for each student.

2. Choose one or more of the following activities for the students, and direct them to find and circle or list all words that fit into that category.

    – words with a given beginning or ending sound

    – words containing a specific blend or vowel sound

    – words containing a vowel sound controlled by "R"

    – four-, five-, six- or seven-letter words

    – words with a specified number of syllables

    – homonyms, antonyms, synonyms, or heteronyms

    – words with double letters

    – words with prefixes or suffixes

    – contractions

    – compound words

    – plurals

    – possessives

    – words rhyming with a word printed on the chalkboard

ADAPTATION

To provide variety, all the above activities and others appropriate to group needs may be printed on cards which are placed in a basket to be passed around so that each student may select one card.

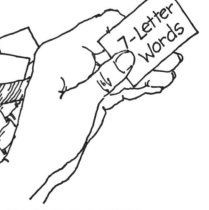

AN INDEX INDICATES

An index is a listing of terms and subject areas which can be found in the backs of some books. The terms are presented in alphabetical order, and the page number on which each item appears is also given. This tool helps a reader who knows the information that he or she is looking for, but cannot find it listed in the table of contents.

Many school books such as history and science texts contain indexes. Other books such as poetry anthologies and biographies also have them. Find several books which have indexes, and study these until you understand index form.

Choose at least 11 of your favorite poems, and copy each on a separate sheet of paper. (Hint: cut regular sheets of paper into halves or quarters, and write one poem on each side of a page.) Number your pages, and make a cover (with the title of your choice) and a table of contents for your book.

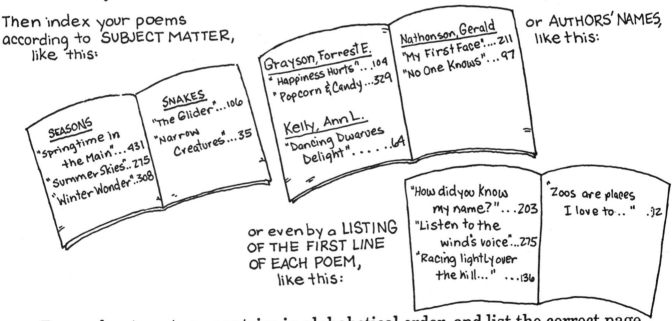

Then index your poems according to SUBJECT MATTER, like this:

SEASONS
"Springtime in the Main"...431
"Summer Skies"..215
"Winter Wonder"..308

SNAKES
"The Glider"...106
"Narrow Creatures"...35

Grayson, Forrest E.
"Happiness Hurts"...104
"Popcorn & Candy...329

Kelly, Ann L.
"Dancing Dwarves Delight".....64

Nathanson, Gerald
"My First Face"....211
"No One Knows"...97

or AUTHORS' NAMES, like this:

or even by a LISTING OF THE FIRST LINE OF EACH POEM, like this:

"How did you know my name?"...203
"Listen to the wind's voice"...275
"Racing lightly over the hill..."...136

"Zoos are places I love to..."...92

Remember to put your entries in alphabetical order, and list the correct page number beside each. Write your index on the last page of your book, add a back cover, and staple or bind your pages together.

Name _____ Date_____

©1994 by INCENTIVE PUBLICATIONS, Inc., Nashville, TN.

❖ GLANCING AT THE GLOSSARY ❖

PURPOSE: Using the glossary

PREPARATION

1. Choose a classroom text with a glossary. Be certain each student has a copy of the text.

2. Divide the class into two teams.

3. Make chalk and a section of the chalkboard available for the game.

PROCEDURE

1. The teacher calls out a word from the glossary.

2. The first student on each team looks through the glossary to find the word, runs to the chalkboard, and writes the word and its definition on the board. The first student to complete the writing receives one point for his or her team.

3. While the first two players are writing on the board, the rest of the players (on both teams) find the word in the glossary, read its meaning, and look through the text to find where the word was actually used. The first player to find the word in the text stands up and, when called on, tells the page number on which the word was found. This player also receives one point for his or her team. (A time limit of one minute should be set for this portion of the activity.)

4. The first team to reach a score of 30 points wins the game.

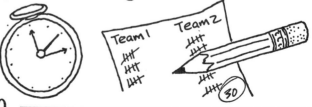

❖ PIN A PLACE ❖

PURPOSE: Using a map to check known facts

PREPARATION

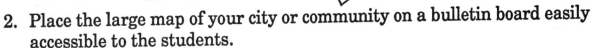

1. Gather the following materials:
   – large map of your community
   – red or yellow yarn
   – straight pins
   – paper
   – scissors
   – colored felt-tipped pins

2. Place the large map of your city or community on a bulletin board easily accessible to the students.

3. Draw a fat red circle around the location of your school. Cut out a tiny paper school building, and print the name of your school on it. Pin the symbol inside the circle.

4. Cut paper into strips, and pin them on the bulletin board next to the map.

5. Reproduce the Pin a Place worksheet (page 62), and place it with the straight pins, yarn, and pens near the bulletin board.

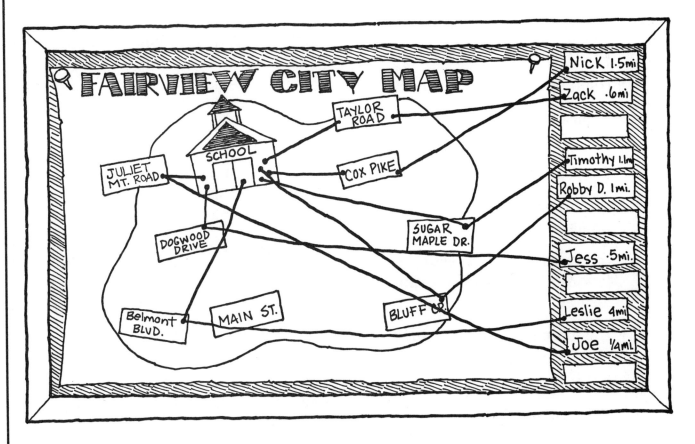

PIN A PLACE

1. Find your street on the map.

2. String a piece of yarn from your street to the school, and from your street to the side of the bulletin board where the sentence strips are pinned.

3. Figure out how far it is from your home to the school. Write your name and the distance on a sentence strip. Attach the end of your piece of yarn to the strip.

4. As you have time, find:

   - your best friend's street

   - all of the streets between your house and the school

   - the street on which the grocery store at which your family shops is located

   - the street on which the post office is located

   - the river nearest to the school

   - the lake closest to your home

   - a park near your home

   - the public library branch nearest your home

   - the fire station closest to your home

   - the street on which your favorite fast food restaurant is located

   - the main street in your town

ALL ABOUT AUSTRALIA

Read about Australia in your encyclopedia or geography book.
Using what you have learned and a map of Australia, complete the following crossword puzzle.

ACROSS

1. The highest mountain in Australia.
3. The state capital of the Northern Territory.
9. The body of water found off the coast of Cairns.
10. The Australian flag has this many stars.
11. If you were traveling from Adelaide to Sydney, in which direction would you go?
13. The longest river in Australia.
14. An island state of Australia south of Melbourne.
15. Ocean off the western coast of Australia.
16. Largest seaport in western Australia.

DOWN

2. Australian city with the largest population.
4. Opposite of "Old North Wales."
5. Australian state with Brisbane as its capital city.
6. Australia is close to the _____ Pole.
7. The capital city of Australia.
8. A state in Australia named for a famous English queen.
12. Australia is not only a country; it is also a _____.

Name _____ Date _____

WORLDLY WISE

Use your globe to complete these sentences.

1. Two European countries which are
   not a part of the European continent are _____

   & _____.

2. The country directly north of the United States is _____.

3. _____ is the European country closest to Africa.

4. _____ is the largest Caribbean island.

5. A country which is also a continent is _____.

6. If you are in Nairobi, Kenya, the nearest ocean to you would be the
   _____.

7. The country directly west of Argentina is _____.

8. The large body of water which separates Europe from Africa is
   _____.

9. The European country which has a shape resembling a boot is _____.

10. North of the Soviet Union there is a body of water called the _____
    Ocean.

11. A large country in Asia of which Beijing is the capital city is _____.

12. The country that shares a border with Norway is _____.

Plan a trip around the world. Write a day-by-day itinerary of your travels
using a globe for help.

Name _____ Date _____

BENJY'S BEST BET

Spring is just around the corner, and Benjy is making plans to buy the mini-bike of his dreams. All winter, he has been saving for the three-horsepower red mini-bike in Mr. Gardner's show window. He has shoveled snow, tended house plants, and run errands to earn money, but he still does not have enough.

He has finally decided to borrow the money and work for Mr. Gardner to pay it back. His problem now is to choose the best of these finance plans.

Charge-A-Card Co.
$40 down payment; $10.50 monthly payments for 1½ years.
Best Credit Union
No down payment; $21.00 monthly payments for 1 year.
Easy Loan Company
$13.50 down payment; $13.50 monthly payment for 13 months.
Trusty Bank Loans
$29.00 down payment; $29.00 monthly payments for 7 months.

Complete this cost chart to help Benjy make his decision.

COST CHART	Monthly Payments	Number of Payments	Down Payment	Total Cost
Charge-A-Card Co.	$_____ x	_____ +	$_____ =	$_____
Best Credit Union	$_____ x	_____ +	$_____ =	$_____
Easy Loan Co.	$_____ x	_____ +	$_____ =	$_____
Trusty Bank Loans.	$_____ x	_____ +	$_____ =	$_____

Draw a star beside the name of the company offering the best finance plan.

Name _____ Date _____

GRAPH GAZING

If you made a graph showing how tall your classmates are, it might look something like this.

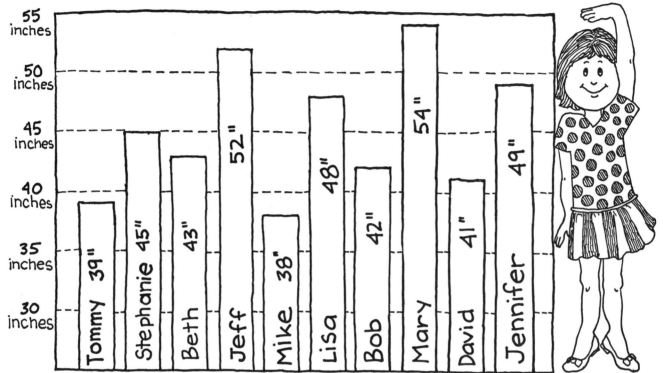

Using this graph, answer the following questions.

1. Which student is tallest? _____

2. How much taller than David is Stephanie? _____

3. If Tommy were 5 inches taller, how tall would he be? _____

4. Bob wants to be as tall as Mary.
   How many more inches does he need to grow? _____

5. If the ceiling is 72 inches high, how many more
   inches could Jeff grow before his head would touch it? _____

6. Lisa is 48 inches tall. How many feet tall is she? _____

7. Which student is the shortest? _____

Use a ruler to measure the heights of six objects in your classroom. Make a graph to show the different heights of the objects. Which is the tallest object? Which is the shortest one?

Name _____ Date _____

LOST IN PUNCTUATION FOREST

Punctuation marks are like trail marks in a forest because they help to guide you through what you read.

Read the story below and supply the missing punctuation marks. Cross out the punctuation symbols shown here as you place them correctly in the story.

. . . .
, ,
! ! ! ! ? ? ? ? ? ? ( ) : : : ; ;
" " " " " " " " " " " " " " " " " " " "

Sound the alarm cried the principal of G S Evram School Our fourth fifth and sixth grade classes are lost in Punctuation Forest Mr Bledsoe Ms Williams and Mrs Kern their teachers took them there on a field trip to search for the marvelous mysterious morning-blooming Comma Trees that grow hidden deep in the woods and they were to be back no later than 11 00 It's nearly 3 00 now Where can they possibly be

All of the teachers had gathered around they wanted to hear what the principal was saying Ms Alexander the principal sounded very upset so the teachers began to discuss what would be the best thing to do Over their voices Mr Guilford called Listen there are two things to remember in an emergency remain calm and think clearly before you act

Mr Alvarez asked Have the police been notified

Yes replied Ms Alexander they've put out an A P B all points bulletin for them over their radios and the C B people have been contacted too

Well in that case declared Mr Alvarez there's nothing to do but wait

Gloom fell over the group they waited worried and listened in silence Suddenly from far away down the street they heard a loud putt-putt-putt and the creaking sound of a bus coming toward the school Was it Could it be Yes It was the missing bus complete with students teachers and driver and armloads of branches from the morning-blooming Comma Trees

Safe at last Ms Alexander sighed with relief as everyone got off the bus Now who is going to explain why you're back so late

Name _____ Date_____

❖ OUTLINES CAN GO AROUND AND AROUND ❖

PURPOSE: Outlining/organizing ideas

PREPARATION

1. Provide the following materials for the students:
   – outline circles
   – pens
   – paper
   – appropriate books
   – reading or content assignment,
     or research projects

2. Reproduce copies of the outline circle on page 69.

3. Prepare two or three circles to use as examples.

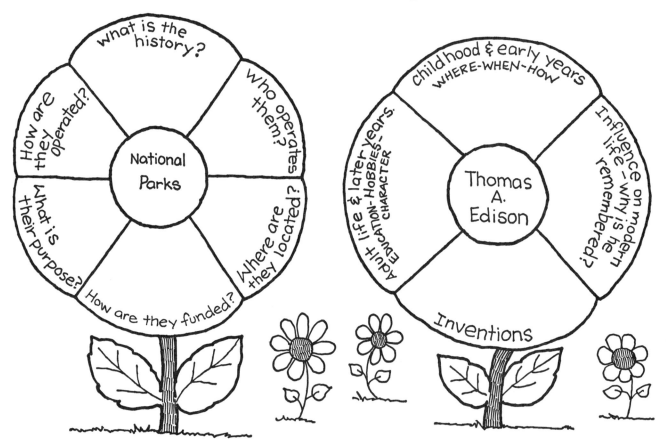

PROCEDURE

1. Write the name of your book, topic, or project in the center of the circle.

2. Decide what the main ideas are, and label the circle sections to help you in gathering and organizing your information.

3. Fill each of the sections with the appropriate information.

OUTLINES CAN GO AROUND AND AROUND

Name _____ Date _____

CONSIDER THE SOURCE

Discover more about a holiday that interests you by researching that holiday and writing a report of your findings. Use at least three different resources (books, magazines, pamphlets, etc.) to learn all you can about its history and development, symbols, traditions, decorations, foods, music, and changes in the methods of celebration over the years. Make careful notes; then write your report.

Resources Used:

1. _____

2. _____

3. _____

Notes (Use another sheet of paper if you need more room to write.)

1. Country where holiday originated_____

2. Time _____

3. Purpose or reason for holiday _____

4. Customs/Rituals _____

   _____

5. Early celebrations _____

   _____

6. Modern-day celebrations _____

   _____

7. Other important information _____

   _____

   Check your notes to be sure you have enough information for an interesting report. If you don't, select a fourth reference book to use.

Name _____ Date_____

©1994 by Incentive Publications, Inc., Nashville, TN.

A QUICK ONCE-OVER

Use a copy of the newspaper to complete this activity.

1. The most important front page news article is about

_____

2. My horoscope for the day is on page _____ .

3. The name of the main character in the most interesting comic strip in the

paper is _____ .

4. A letter to the editor that interested me is about_____

_____

_____

I (agree/disagree) _____ with the writer's opinion.

5. According to the weather forecast,
   we should expect tomorrow to be a
   _____day.

6. After consulting the television schedule for this evening, I have found
   _____ programs that I might watch. The one
   I especially want to see will be shown at
   _____ o'clock on Channel _____ .

7. This is a picture of an object that I would like
   to own which is advertised by _____
   Co. The price is _____ .

Name _____ Date_____

AN INSIDE LOOK AT BOOKS

Think about all the books you have read or hope to read in the near future. Use the card catalog or other resources to help you complete this activity.

1. If I could take only one book on a long journey,

   I would take _____

   because_____

   _____

   _____ .

MY FAVORITE BOOK BY Leslie B.

2. The book I would choose to share with a friend from another country would

   be _____

   because _____

   _____ .

3. _____ is an author whose books I enjoy.

   The thing I like best about the books he or she writes is _____

   _____ .

4. The most beautiful picture book I've ever seen is _____

   _____ .

   The illustrations are _____

   _____ .

5. Right now, I am really enjoying reading books about _____

   _____ .

Name _____ Date _____

©1994 by Incentive Publications, Inc., Nashville, TN.

AN INSIDE LOOK AT BOOKS

6. Here is a three-line review of a book I've just read.

Title of Book: _____

Review: _____

_____

_____

_____

7. _____ is a book

that I didn't enjoy. The main thing I disliked about this book was _____

_____

_____ .

8. If I had a lot of money to buy books for presents, I would buy _____

_____ for my teacher,

_____ for _____

_____ , and for my own library, I would buy

_____ .

Fasten these two pages together so that the blank sides of the paper form the outsides. Design and color an attractive cover. Print a title and your name as author on the front. Use the back cover to list the books you read during the next month.

Name _____ Date_____

©1994 by Incentive Publications, Inc., Nashville, TN.

ON THE LOOKOUT FOR WORDS

Good readers are always on the lookout for new words to add to their speaking, reading, and writing vocabularies.

As you read this week, add words to this list that you did not know before.

Learn The Meaning For Reading	Need To Be Able To Spell For Writing	Learn And Use In Conversation

Name _____ Date_____

1. Circle all of the books you would read for pleasure.

2. Make stripes on the books you would use to help you become a better student.

3. Draw a triangle around the books you would look through occasionally for information related to a specific topic.

4. Make polka dots on the books you would skim through from time to time, but would probably never sit down to read all the way through.

5. Draw stars on the books you would need to read very carefully for important details.

6. Write the names of three special books from your own library shelf on the blank books.

Name _____ Date_____

READING KNOW-HOW

Increase your reading know-how! Match these reading terms with their correct meanings.

Reading Terms	**Meanings**
a. Abbreviation	___ 1. a word that has the same spelling as another word, but is pronounced differently and has a different meaning. *Example: wind – wind*
b. Antonym	___ 2. a letter or group of letters pronounced either as a part of a word or a whole word.
c. Compound Word	___ 3. a shortened form of a word which usually ends with a period. *Example: Mister – Mr.*
d. Consonant	___ 4. any of the letters a, e, i, o, and u (and sometimes y) in the English alphabet. Every word or syllable must contain at least one.
e. Contraction	___ 5. a word formed by combining two separate words to create a new word. *Example: snowflake*
f. Heteronym	___ 6. a set of letters placed before a root word to form a word with a new meaning. *Example: unhappy*
g. Homonym	___ 7. a word from which other words are formed by adding a prefix and/or a suffix. *Example: repaint, raining*
h. Prefix	___ 8. a word that means the opposite of a given word. *Example: hot – cold*
i. Rhyming Word	___ 9. a word formed by joining two words together but leaving out one (or more) of the letters and replacing it (or them) with an apostrophe. *Example: are not – aren't*
j. Root Word	___10. a word that has an ending sound which sounds like the ending of another word. *Example: pail – mail*
k. Suffix	___11. a word that has a meaning similar to, or the same as, another word. *Example: sick – ill*
l. Syllable	___12. the letters b, c, d, f, g, h, j, k, l, m, n, p, q, r, s, t, v, w, x, y, and z of the English alphabet.
m. Synonym	___13. a letter or syllable placed at the end of a root word to form a word with a new meaning. *Example: highest*
n. Vowel	___14. a word that sounds like another word, but that has a different meaning and a different spelling. *Example: pair – pear*

Name _____   Date_____

Author's Savvy, page 9

When Alicia <u>realized</u> that she was <u>alone</u> in the <u>vacant</u> <u>mansion</u>, her heart began to <u>pound</u>. She <u>screamed</u> for help, but her only <u>reply</u> was an <u>eerie</u> <u>silence</u>. Her <u>footsteps</u> <u>reverberated</u> as she <u>crept</u> through the <u>deserted</u> hallway to the <u>head</u> of the stairs. She <u>paused</u> and tried to <u>peer</u> through the <u>shadowy</u> <u>mist</u> that filled the <u>abode</u> to see what was at the <u>foot</u> of the <u>staircase</u>, but everything was <u>indistinct</u>. Her legs <u>trembled</u> as she <u>forced</u> herself <u>to descend</u> the stairs. When she <u>reached</u> the landing, she <u>sank</u> down to rest. She was too <u>frightened</u> to go <u>farther</u>. <u>Suddenly</u> something <u>ghostly</u> moved at the <u>base</u> of the <u>steps</u>. Alicia was too <u>terrified</u> to <u>breathe</u>. She heard something <u>moving</u> toward her, something that had <u>pointed</u> <u>nails</u> that clicked on <u>each</u> step. She <u>shrank</u> against the <u>banister</u>. Whatever it was had <u>almost</u> <u>discovered</u> her. She heard a <u>low</u> <u>snarl</u> and felt something <u>icy</u> <u>trail</u> over her arm. <u>Fearing</u> the worst, she <u>peeked</u> up <u>at last</u>, and then <u>held</u> out her arms. A warm <u>fuzzy</u> body climbed into her lap and <u>nuzzled</u> her shoulder. Alicia <u>giggled</u> out loud. It was her own <u>puppy</u> Oscar. She wasn't <u>isolated</u> anymore. She and Oscar <u>jumped</u> up and <u>raced</u> down the rest of the <u>stairway</u> and out the front door into the <u>sunshine</u>. They were <u>safe</u> at last!

Author's Savvy II, page 10

As the <u>caravan</u> went into the <u>dense</u> jungle for a nine-day <u>safari</u>, they were <u>startled</u> to hear a <u>tremendous</u> <u>snarl</u> coming from behind a <u>huge</u> tree. The leader <u>rushed</u> <u>forward</u> to find himself <u>peering</u> into the <u>glowing</u> eyes of a <u>hostile</u> and <u>ferocious</u> tiger with a <u>cavernous</u> mouth, <u>razor-edged</u> teeth, and a <u>ravenous</u> look about it. With one quick <u>pounce</u> and a <u>deafening</u> <u>roar</u>, the tiger <u>devoured</u> the leader. Deciding that the man was a <u>delicious</u> <u>morsel</u>, the tiger <u>sniffed</u> the air, looking for more people to <u>consume</u>. Following the <u>scent</u>, he <u>sped</u> straight toward the <u>frightened</u> <u>travelers</u> to <u>continue</u> his <u>feast</u>. Acting <u>swiftly</u>, a man <u>grabbed</u> a <u>rifle</u> and <u>aimed</u> it at the tiger. He <u>squeezed</u> the trigger, and there was a <u>resounding</u> <u>explosion</u>! Smoke <u>filled</u> the air. When it <u>cleared</u>, the <u>trembling</u> people <u>scanned</u> the <u>area</u> where the tiger had been. They were <u>amazed</u> to see nothing there. All that <u>remained</u> of the tiger was a <u>golden</u> and <u>cinnamon</u> striped hammock <u>hanging</u> between two trees. "Oh, dear," <u>sighed</u> the man. "What I was <u>shooting</u> for was a tiger-skin <u>rug</u>!"

A Tragic Tale, page 11

Mistress Evans, who lives in the Tower **Apartment Building** on Centennial **Boulevard**, fell down the stairs and broke her leg. Her neighbor, **Mister** Bradley, was nearby and immediately telephoned **Doctor** Tugwell at his office on **West Main Street**. Since it was **Monday morning, September first**, the office was closed and everyone was on holiday.

Thinking quickly, **Mister** Bradley dialed the number for **Saint** Andrews Hospital on Westchester **Avenue** and asked for the Emergency **Department**. He explained the situation to a nurse, who said, "Tell **Mistress** Evans that an ambulance from Hospital Helpers, **Incorporated** is leaving now to pick her up and bring her here."

Mistress Evans was relieved to know that help was on the way, but she was still very angry. She said, "It's the **building superintendent's** fault! If he had fixed that broken step three **weeks** ago when we reported it, none of this would have happened. I'm going to call my **attorney**!"

Just then, **Captain** Norton of Ships, International came up the stairs. "Avast there, you lubbers," he boomed, "you look like a ship stuck on a sandbar! What's the problem?"

Mister Bradley told **Captain** Norton what had happened, and **Mistress** Evans repeated her plans to contact her **attorney**. The **captain** nodded his head sympathetically and said, "Tell your **attorney** to contact the Sunshine Realty **Company** at 29 **South** Watley **Court**. They own this **building**."

Suddenly, three people in white uniforms carrying a stretcher over seven **feet** long entered the stairwell. **Captain** Norton exclaimed, "Right this way . . . right up here! Hurry—we've been waiting for at least an **hour**, and this lady's leg is as swollen as a **gallon** jug! Look lively there! You've wasted five **minutes** just staring! What you need is six **months** in the Navy to teach you to move!"

The ambulance attendants ran up the stairs, put **Mistress** Evans on the stretcher, and bundled her into the ambulance. As they drove away, **Mister** Bradley shook his head and said, "Poor **Mistress** Evans. It's too bad that she had to start the Fall with a fall!"

Plural Decisions, page 13

True statements to be shaded in are:
1, 2, 4, 7, 9

Positively Possessives, page 14

Sentences using the possessive apostrophe are: 1, 4, 5, 7, 10, 12

Hettie Harnesses Heteronyms, page 15

1. read/read
3. tear/tear
2. live/live
4. record/record

The Meaning of Math, page 16

1. triangle
2. percent
3. graph
4. multiplication
5. quotient
6. zero
7. square
8. average
9. product
10. subtraction

Show Your Feelings, page 22

Bewildered
Happy
Irritated
Embarrassed
Frightened
Wicked
Mournful
Glamorous
Delighted
Quiet
Jealous
Sick

Pressed
Bitter
Weak
Gloomy
Joyful
Confident
Friendly
Calm
Grumpy
Tense
Annoyed
Cheerful

Suspicious
Thoughtful
Agreeable
Pleased
Generous
Upset
Sad
Weary
Lonely
Dejected
Lax

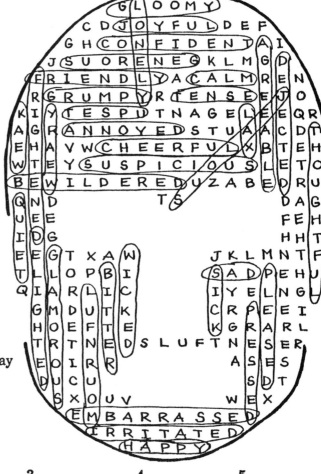

Peering at Paragraphs, page 29

Paragraph 1: Spring had finally arrived.
Paragraph 2: The storm we had been waiting for all day finally broke.
Paragraph 3: "I've looked everywhere for that book!"
Paragraph 4: It was time for the party to begin.

Detail Deduction, page 30

	1.	2.	3.	4.	5.
Who:	the little girl	many people	Julie	Danny, the dog	the family
What:	looking for shells & rocks	work	laughed	barked	searched
Where:	walking along the beach	in hotels	at the circus	outside the gate	the forest
How:	carefully	very hard	loudly	wildly	bravely
Why:	for her collection	in order to gain experience	because she had been entertained by the clown	to signal the stranger's arrival	because of their concern for the lost child
When:	at dusk	while they are in management school	after school	midnight	all day long

Analogies on Deposit, page 31

1. shell	5. money	9. hand	13. black
2. knife	6. finger	10. meadow	14. earth
3. tree	7. seashore	11. airplane	15. box
4. fish	8. ladder	12. carpenter	16. dog

Identify the Irrelevants, page 42

Paragraph 1: My mother said we were going to have hamburgers for dinner.

Paragraph 2: Richard's sister Cheryl dropped her doll and began to cry.

Paragraph 3: Percival's favorite color is green.

Paragraph 4: I don't know how to whistle.

Relevant References, page 51

ACROSS
2. calendar
5. telephone book
9. card catalog
10. map
11. encyclopedia

DOWN
1. magazine
3. newspaper
4. cookbook
5. thesaurus
6. dictionary
7. catalog
8. atlas

Card Catalog Cogitation, pgs 56-57

1. T	4. F	7. F	10. F	13. F
2. F	5. F	8. T	11. T	
3. T	6. T	9. T	12. F	

All About Australia, page 63

ACROSS
1. Kosciusko
3. Darwin
9. Coral Sea
10. six
11. East
13. Murray
14. Tasmania
15. Indian
16. Perth

DOWN
2. Sydney
4. New South Wales
5. Queensland
6. South
7. Canberra
8. Victoria
12. Continent

Worldly Wise, page 64

1. United Kingdom & Ireland	7. Chile
2. Canada	8. Mediterranean
3. Spain	9. Italy
4. Cuba	10. Arctic
5. Australia	11. China
6. Indian	12. Sweden

Graph Gazing, page 66

1. Mary	3. 44"	5. 20"	7. Mike
2. 4"	4. 12"	6. 4'	

Lost in Punctuation Forest, page 67

"Sound the alarm!" cried the principal of G. S. Evram School. "Our fourth, fifth, and sixth grade classes are lost in Punctuation Forest! Mr. Bledsoe, Ms. Williams, and Mrs. Kern, their teachers, took them there on a field trip to search for the marvelous, mysterious, morning-blooming Comma Trees that grow hidden deep in the woods, and they were to be back no later than 11:00. It's nearly 3:00 now! Where can they possibly be?"

All of the teachers had gathered around; they wanted to hear what the principal was saying. Ms. Alexander, the principal, sounded very upset, so the teachers began to discuss what would be the best thing to do. Over their voices Mr. Guilford called, "Listen, there are two things to remember in an emergency: remain calm, and think clearly before you act."

Mr. Alvarez asked, "Have the police been notified?"

"Yes," replied Ms. Alexander, "they've put out an A.P.B. (all points bulletin) for them over their radios, and the C.B. people have been contacted, too."

"Well, in that case," declared Mr. Alvarez, "there's nothing to do but wait."

Gloom fell over the group; they waited, worried, and listened in silence. Suddenly, from far away down the street, they heard a loud putt-putt-putt and the creaking sound of a bus coming toward the school. Was it? Could it be? Yes! It was the missing bus, complete with students, teachers, and driver, and armloads of branches from the morning-blooming Comma Trees.

"Safe at last," Ms. Alexander sighed with relief as everyone got off the bus. "Now, who is going to explain why you're back so late?"

Reading Know-How, page 76

1. f	3. a	5. c	7. j	9. e	11. m	13. k
2. l	4. n	6. h	8. b	10. i	12. d	14. g